GW01377223

Master Your Traeger Grill Wood Pellet Grill Smoker

Tailor Made Program To Understanding How The Wood Pellet Smoker And Grill Works Plus Tasty Recipes For The Perfect Bbq.

Written By

MICHAEL BLACKWOOD

© Copyright 2021 - All rights reserved.

The content contained within this book may not be reproduced, duplicated or transmitted without direct written permission from the author or the publisher.

Under no circumstances will any blame or legal responsibility be held against the publisher, or author, for any damages, reparation, or monetary loss due to the information contained within this book. Either directly or indirectly.

Legal Notice:

This book is copyright protected. This book is only for personal use. You cannot amend, distribute, sell, use, quote or paraphrase any part, or the content within this book, without the consent of the author or publisher.

Disclaimer Notice:

Please note the information contained within this document is for educational and entertainment purposes only. All effort has been executed to present accurate, up to date, and reliable, complete information. No warranties of any kind are declared or implied. Readers acknowledge that the author is not engaging in the rendering of legal, financial, medical or professional advice. The content within this book has been derived from various sources. Please consult a licensed professional before attempting any techniques outlined in this book.

By reading this document, the reader agrees that under no circumstances is the author responsible for any losses, direct or indirect, which are incurred as a result of the use of information contained within this document, including, but not limited to, — errors, omissions, or inaccuracies.

Table of Contents

- PART 1 – *9*

WOOD PELLET SMOKER COOKBOOK *9*

BARBECUE *11*

    Cajun Barbecue Chicken 12

APPETIZERS AND SIDES *15*

    Bacon Cheddar Slider 16

    Apple Wood Smoked Cheese 18

    Hickory Smoked Moink Ball Skewer 20

BEEF *23*

    George's Smoked Tri-Tip 24

    Pulled Beef 26

    Smoked Roast Beef 28

    Smoked Beef Ribs 30

LAMB *31*

    Lamb Rack Wrapped In Apple Wood Walnut 32

    Roasted Lamb Leg 34

    Greek Leg of Lamb 36

CHICKEN *39*

    Pineapple Cinnamon Smoked Chicken Thighs 40

    Wood Pellet Smoked Chicken Breasts 42

    Delicious Chicken Fritters 44

    Wood Pellet Grilled Chicken Satay 47

TURKEY *49*

    Turkey Breast _____ 50

    Apple wood-Smoked Whole Turkey _____ 53

PORK _____ 55

    Apple Wood Paprika Chili Smoked Pulled Pork _____ 56

    Bourbon Honey Glazed Smoked Pork Ribs _____ 59

    Lime Barbecue Smoked Pork Shoulder Chili _____ 61

    Chili Sweet Smoked Pork Tenderloin _____ 64

    Gingery Maple Glazed Smoked Pork Ribs_____ 66

    Tasty Grilled Pork Chops _____ 68

    Delicious Barbeque and Grape Jelly Pork Chops _____ 70

    Bacon Wrapped Jalapeno Poppers _____ 72

    Barbeque Baby Back Ribs _____ 74

    Delicious Grilled Pulled Pork_____ 76

DESSERT _____ 79

    Cheesy Jalapeño Skillet Dip _____ 80

    Cajun Turkey Club_____ 82

RUBS, SAUCES, MARINADES, AND GLAZES _____ 85

    Three Pepper Rub _____ 86

    Jerky Seasoning _____ 87

    Not-Just-For-Pork Rub _____ 89

    Chicken Rub_____ 90

- PART 2 -_____ 91

ELECTRIC SMOKER COOKBOOK _____ 91

APPETIZERS, VEGETABLES, AND SIDES _____ 93

    Twice-Baked Spaghetti Squash _____ 94

    Bacon-Wrapped Asparagus_____ 97

Garlic Parmesan Wedges _____ 99

BEEF _____ 103

Savory Smoked Beef Chuck Roast with Red Wine Sauce 104

Butter Garlic Smoked Beef Rib Eye Rosemary _____ 107

Oak-Smoked Top Round _____ 110

LAMB _____ 113

Garlic Mint Smoked Lamb Chops Balsamic _____ 114

CHICKEN _____ 117

American Style Chicken Thighs _____ 118

Smoked Chicken Cutlets In Strawberries-Balsamic Marinade _____ 120

Beer Can Chicken _____ 122

TURKEY _____ 125

Turkey with Chimichurri _____ 126

PORK _____ 129

Smoked Boston Butt Roast _____ 130

Smoked Pork Shoulder _____ 132

Smoked Pork Sausage _____ 134

SEAFOOD _____ 136

Smoked Red Fish Fillets _____ 137

Lemon Pepper Tuna _____ 140

Seasoned Shrimp Skewers _____ 142

RUBS, SAUCES, MARINADES, AND GLAZES _____ 144

Mustard Sauce for Pork _____ 145

- 1 cup yellow mustard _____ 145
- ½ cup balsamic vinegar _____ 145

- 1/3 cup brown sugar _____145
- 2 tablespoons butter _____145
- 1 tablespoon fresh lemon juice _____145
- 2 teaspoons Worcestershire sauce_____145
- ½ teaspoon chili powder _____145

Spicy-Citrus Cocktail Sauce_____147

– PART 1 –

WOOD PELLET SMOKER COOKBOOK

Internal Design of the Wood Pellet Smoke and Grill

Modern designs of Wood Pellet Smoker-Grills contain electronic functionality. Advanced design allows smoker-grills to manage temperature control and pellets on its own. The wood pellets are transferred to the burning area according to the cooking setting you provide. The one push of a button, you can allow the smoker-grill to take care of the temperature consistency and the flavors of the food inside.

BARBECUE

Cajun Barbecue Chicken

Preparation Time: 15 minutes
Cooking Time: 25 minutes
Servings: 4

Ingredients:

- 2 tablespoons sweet spicy dry rub
- 1/4 teaspoon ground thyme
- 1/2 teaspoon oregano
- 1 tablespoon olive oil
- 1 lb. chicken breast fillet
- 2 cloves garlic clove, minced
- 1/2 cup barbecue sauce
- 1 tablespoon butter
- 1/4 cup beer

- 1 tablespoon Worcestershire sauce
- 1 tablespoon lime juice
- 1 teaspoon hot sauce

Directions:

1. Combine the dry rub, thyme and oregano in a bowl.
2. Coat the chicken breasts with olive oil.
3. Season both sides with the dry rub mixture.
4. Set the wood pellet grill to 350 degrees F.
5. Add the chicken breast to the grill.
6. Grill for 7 to 8 minutes.
7. Let rest for 10 minutes.
8. Combine rest of the ingredients in a saucepan. Bring to a boil.
9. Serve the chicken with the sauce.

Nutrition: Calories: 286 Carbs: 14g Fat: 5g Protein: 38g

APPETIZERS AND SIDES

Bacon Cheddar Slider

Preparation Time: 30 Minutes
Cooking Time: 15 Minutes
Servings: 6 To 10

Ingredients:

- 1 pound ground beef (80% lean)
- ½ teaspoon of garlic salt
- ½ teaspoon salt
- ½ teaspoon of garlic
- ½ teaspoon onion
- ½ teaspoon black pepper
- 6 bacon slices, cut in half
- ½ Cup mayonnaise
- 2 teaspoons of creamy wasabi (optional)
- 6 sliced sharp cheddar cheese, cut in half (optional)
- Sliced red onion
- ½ Cup sliced kosher dill pickles
- 12 mini breads sliced horizontally
- Ketchup

Directions:

1. Place ground beef, garlic salt, seasoned salt, garlic powder, onion powder and black hupe pepper in a medium bowl.

2. Divide in 12 equal parts the meat mixture into shape into small thin round patties (about 2 ounces each) and save.
3. Cook the bacon on medium heat over medium heat for 5-8 minutes until crunchy. Set aside.
4. To make the sauce, mix the mayonnaise and horseradish in a small bowl, if used.
5. Set up a wood pellet smoker and grill for direct cooking to use griddle accessories. Look for the manufacturer to see if there is a griddle accessory that works with the particular wooden pellet smoker and grill.
6. Spray a cooking spray on the griddle cooking surface for best non-stick results.
7. Preheat wood pellet smoker and grill to 350 ° F using selected pellets. Griddle surface should be approximately 400 ° F.
8. Grill the putty for 3-4 minutes each until the internal temperature reaches 160 ° F.
9. If necessary, place a sharp cheddar cheese slice on each patty while the patty is on the griddle or after the patty is removed from the griddle. Place a small amount of mayonnaise mixture, a slice of red onion, and a hamburger pate in the lower half of each roll. Pickled slices, bacon and ketchup

Nutrition: Calories: 80 Carbs: 0g Fat: 5g Protein: 0g

Apple Wood Smoked Cheese

Preparation Time: 1 Hour 15 Minutes

Cooking Time: 2 Hours

Servings: 6

Ingredients:

- Gouda
- Sharp cheddar
- Very sharp 3 year cheddar
- Monterey Jack
- Pepper jack
- Swiss

Directions:

1. According to the shape of the cheese block, cut the cheese block into an easy-to-handle size (approximately 4 x 4 inch block) to promote smoke penetration.
2. Leave the cheese on the counter for one hour to form a very thin skin or crust, which acts as a heat barrier, but allows smoke to penetrate.
3. Configure the wood pellet smoking grill for indirect heating and install a cold smoke box to prepare for cold smoke. Make sure that the louvers on the smoking box are fully open to allow moisture to escape from the box.
4. Preheat the wood pellet smoker and grill to 180 °F or use apple pellets and smoke settings, if any, to get a milder smoke flavor.
5. Place the cheese on a Teflon-coated fiberglass non-stick grill mat and let cool for 2 hours.
6. Remove the smoked cheese and cool for 1 hour on the counter using a cooling rack.
7. After labelling the smoked cheese with a vacuum seal, refrigerate for 2 weeks or more, then smoke will permeate and the cheese flavor will become milder.

Nutrition: Calories: 102 Carbs: 0g Fat: 9g Protein: 6g

Hickory Smoked Moink Ball Skewer

Preparation Time: 30 Minutes

Cooking Time: 1 Hour 30 Minutes

Servings: 9

Ingredients:

- ½ pound ground beef (80% lean)
- ½ pound pork sausage
- 1 large egg
- ½ cup Italian bread crumbs
- ½ cup chopped red onion
- Grated parmesan cheese cup
- ¼ Cup finely chopped parsley
- ¼ cup whole milk
- 2 pieces of garlic, 1 chopped or crushed garlic
- 1 teaspoon oregano
- ½ teaspoon kosher salt
- ½ teaspoon black pepper
- ¼ cup barbecue sauce like Sweet Baby Ray
- ½ pound bacon cut in half, cut in half

Directions:

1. In a container, mix ground beef, ground pork sausage, eggs, crumbs, onions, parmesan cheese, parsley, milk, garlic,

2. salt, oregano, and pepper. Do not overuse the meat.
3. Form a 1½ ounces meatball about 1.5 inches in diameter and place on a Teflon-coated fiberglass mat.
4. Wrap each meatball in half thin bacon. Stab moink balls on 6 skewers (3 balls per skewer).
5. Set up wood pellet smoker and grill for indirect cooking.
6. Preheat wood pellet smoker and grill to 225 ° F using hickory pellets.
7. Tap the moink ball skewer for 30 minutes.
8. Raise the pit temperature to 350 ° F until the meatball internal temperature reaches 175 ° F and the bacon is crisp (about 40-45 minutes).
9. For the last 5 minutes, brush your moink ball with your favorite barbecue sauce.
10. While still hot, offer moink ball skewers.

Nutrition: Calories: 170 Carbs: 2g Fat: 15g Protein: 7g

BEEF

George's Smoked Tri-Tip

Preparation Time: 25 minutes

Cooking Time: 5 hours

Servings: 4

Ingredients:

- 1½ pounds tri-tip roast
- Salt
- Freshly ground black pepper
- 2 teaspoons garlic powder
- 2 teaspoons lemon pepper
- ½ cup apple juice

Directions:

1. Supply your smoker with wood pellets and follow the manufacturer's specific start-up procedure. Allow your grill to preheat with the lid closed, to 180°F.
2. Season the tri-tip roast with salt, pepper, garlic powder, and lemon pepper. Using your two hands, work on the seasoning into the meat.
3. Place the meat to roast directly on the grill grate and smoke for 4 hours.
4. Pull the tri-tip from the grill and place it on enough aluminium foil to wrap it completely.

5. Increase the grill's temperature to 375°F.
6. Fold in three sides of the foil around the roast and add the apple juice. Fold in the last side, completely enclosing the tri-tip and liquid. Return the wrapped tri-tip to the grill and cook for 45 minutes more.
7. Remove the tri-tip roast from the grill and let it rest for 10 to 15 minutes, before unwrapping, slicing, and serving.

Pulled Beef

Preparation Time: 25 minutes

Cooking Time: 12 to 14 hours

Servings: 5 to 8

Ingredients:

- 1 (4-pound) top round roast
- 2 tablespoons yellow mustard
- 1 batch Espresso Brisket Rub
- ½ cup beef broth

Directions:

1. Supply your smoker with wood pellets and follow the manufacturer's specific start-up procedure. Allow your griller to preheat with the lid closed to have a quality food to 225°F.
2. Coat the top round roast all over with mustard and season it with the rub. Using your two hands, work the rub into the meat.
3. Place the meat to roast directly on the grill grate and smoke until its internal temperature reaches 160°F and a dark bark has formed.
4. Pull the roast from the grill and place it on enough aluminum foil to wrap it completely.
5. Increase the grill's temperature to 350°F.
6. Fold in three sides of the foil around the roast and add the beef broth. Fold in the last side, completely enclosing the roast and liquid. Return the wrapped roast to the grill and cook until its internal temperature reaches 195°F.
7. Pull the roast from the grill and place it in a cooler. Cover the cooler and let the roast rest for 1 or 2 hrs.
8. Remove your roast from the cooler and unwrap it. Pull apart the beef using just your fingers. Serve immediately.

Nutrition: Calories: 213 Carbs: 0g Fat: 16g Protein: 15g

Smoked Roast Beef

Preparation Time: 10 minutes

Cooking Time: 12 to 14 hours

Servings: 5 to 8

Ingredients:

- 1 (4-pound) top round roast
- 1 batch Espresso Brisket Rub
- 1 tablespoon butter

Directions:

1. Supply your smoker with wood pellets and follow the manufacturer's specific start-up procedure. Allow your griller to preheat with the lid closed, to 180°F.
2. Season the top round roast with the rub. Using your two hands, work the rub into the meat.
3. Place the meat to roast directly on the grill grate and smoke until its internal temperature reaches 140°F. Remove the roast from the grill.
4. Place a cast-iron skillet on the grill grate and increase the grill's temperature to 450°F. Place the roast in the skillet, add the butter, and cook until its internal temperature reaches 145°F, flipping once after about 3 minutes. (I recommend reverse-

searing the meat over an open flame rather than in the cast-iron skillet, if your grill has that option.)
5. Remove the food you roast from the grill and let it rest for 10 to 15 minutes, before slicing and serving.

Nutrition: Calories: 290 Carbs: 3g Fat: 9g Protein: 50g

Smoked Beef Ribs

Preparation Time: 25 minutes

Cooking Time: 4 to 6 hours

Servings: 4 to 8

Ingredients:

- 2 (2- or 3-pound) racks beef ribs
- 2 tablespoons yellow mustard
- 1 batch Sweet and Spicy Cinnamon Rub

Directions:

1. Supply your smoker with wood pellets and follow the manufacturer's specific start-up procedure. Allow your griller to preheat with the lid closed, to 225°F.
2. Take off the membrane from the backside of the ribs. This can be done by cutting just through the membrane in an X pattern and working a paper towel between the membrane and the ribs to pull it off.
3. Coat the ribs all over with mustard and season them with the rub. Using your two hands, work with the rub into the meat.
4. Put your ribs directly on the grill grate and smoke until their internal temperature reaches between 190°F and 200°F.
5. Remove the racks from the grill and cut them into individual ribs. Serve immediately.

Nutrition: Calories: 230 Carbs: 0g Fat: 17g Protein: 20g

LAMB

Lamb Rack Wrapped In Apple Wood Walnut

Preparation Time: 25 Minutes
Cooking Time: 60 to 90 Minutes
Servings: 4

Ingredients:
- 3 tablespoons of Dijon mustard
- 2 pieces of garlic, chopped or 2 cups of crushed garlic
- ½ teaspoon of garlic
- ½ teaspoon kosher salt
- ½ teaspoon black pepper
- ½ teaspoon rosemary
- 1 (1½ pound) ram rack, French
- 1 cup crushed walnut

Directions:
1. Put mustard, garlic, garlic powder, salt, pepper and rosemary in a small bowl.
2. Spread the seasoning mix evenly on all sides of the lamb and sprinkle with crushed walnuts. Lightly press the walnuts by hand to attach the nuts to the meat.

3. Wrap the walnut-coated lamb rack loosely in plastic wrap and refrigerate overnight to allow the seasoning to penetrate the meat.
4. Remove the walnut-covered lamb rack from the refrigerator and let it rest for 30 minutes to reach room temperature.
5. Set the wood pellet r grill for indirect cooking and preheat to 225 ° F using apple pellets.
6. Lay the grill directly on the rack with the lamb bone down.
7. Smoke at 225 ° F until the thickest part of the ram rack reaches the desired internal temperature. This is measured with a digital instantaneous thermometer near the time listed on the chart.
8. Place the mutton under a loose foil tent for 5 minutes before eating

Nutrition: Calories: 165 Carbs: 0g Fat: 8g Protein: 20g

Roasted Lamb Leg

Preparation Time: 20 Minutes
Cooking Time: 1.5 Hours to 2 Hours
Servings: 6

Ingredients:
- 1 boneless leg of a lamb
- ½ cup of roasted garlic flavored extra virgin olive oil
- ¼ cup dried parsley
- 3 garlics, chopped
- 2 tablespoons of a fresh lemon juice or 1 tablespoon of lemon zest (from 1 medium lemon)
- 2 tablespoons of dried oregano
- 1 tablespoon dried rosemary
- ½ teaspoon black pepper

Directions:
1. Remove the net from the lamb's leg. Cut off grease, silver skin, and large pieces of fat.
2. In a small bowl, mix olive oil, parsley, garlic, lemon juice or zest, oregano, rosemary, and pepper.
3. Spice the inside and outside surfaces of the lamb's boneless legs.

4. Secure the boneless lamb leg using a silicone food band or butcher twine. Use a band or twine to form and maintain the basic shape of the lamb
5. Wrap the lamb loosely in plastic wrap and refrigerate overnight to allow the seasoning to penetrate the meat.
6. Remove the rum from the refrigerator and leave at room temperature for 1 hour.
7. Set up a wood pellet smoker and grill for indirect cooking and preheat to 400 ° F using selected pellets.
8. Remove the wrap from the ram.
9. Insert a wood pellet smoker and grill meat probe or remote meat probe into the thickest part of the lamb. If your grill does not have a meat probe or you do not have a remote meat probe, use an instant reading digital thermometer to read the internal temperature while cooking. Roast the lamb at 400 ° F until the internal temperature of the thickest part reaches the desired finish.
10. Place the lamb under the loose foil tent for 10 minutes, then cut it against the grain and eat.

Nutrition: Calories: 200 Carbs: 1g Fat: 13g Protein: 20g

Greek Leg of Lamb

Preparation Time: 15 minutes
Cooking Time: 25 minutes
Servings: 6

Ingredients:
- 2 tablespoons finely chopped fresh rosemary
- 1 tablespoon ground thyme
- 5 garlic cloves, minced
- 2 tablespoons sea salt
- 1 tablespoon freshly ground black pepper
- Butcher's string
- 1 whole boneless (6- to 8-pound) leg of lamb
- ¼ cup extra-virgin olive oil
- 1 cup red wine vinegar
- ½ cup canola oil

Directions:
1. In a container, combine the rosemary, thyme, garlic, salt, and pepper; set aside.
2. Using butcher's string, tie the leg of lamb into the shape of a roast. Your butcher should also be happy to truss the leg for you.

3. Rub the lamb generously with the olive oil and season with the spice mixture. Put it to a plate, cover with plastic wrap, and refrigerate for 4 hours.
4. Remove the lamb from the refrigerator but do not rinse.
5. Supply your smoker with wood pellets and follow the manufacturer's specific start-up procedure. Preheat, with the lid closed, to 325°F.
6. In a small bowl, combine the red wine vinegar and canola oil for basting.
7. Place the lamb directly on the grill, close the lid, and smoke for 20 to 25 minutes per pound (depending on desired doneness), basting with the oil and vinegar mixture every 30 minutes. Lamb is generally served medium-rare to medium, so it will be done when a meat thermometer where inserted in the thickest part reads 140°F to 145°F.
8. Let the lamb meat rest for about 15 minutes before slicing to serve.

Nutrition: Calories: 130 Carbs: 2g Fat: 5g Protein: 19g

CHICKEN

Pineapple Cinnamon Smoked Chicken Thighs

Preparation Time: 10 minutes
Cooking Time: 1 hour 15 minutes
Servings: 8

Ingredients:
- Chicken thighs (3-lb., 1.4-kg.)
- The Marinade
- 1 ½ cups Ketchup
- 2 cups Pineapple chunks
- ½ cup White vinegar
- 2 teaspoons Garlic powder
- 3 tablespoons Olive oil
- 2 teaspoons Dried thyme
- 1 teaspoon Allspice
- 2 teaspoons Ground cinnamon
- 1 ½ teaspoons Cayenne powder
- ¾ teaspoons Salt

Directions:
1. Place ketchup, pineapple chunks, white vinegar, garlic powder, dried thyme, allspice, ground cinnamon, cayenne

powder, and salt in a food processor then drizzle olive oil over the spices. Process until smooth.
2. Transfer the mixture to a saucepan then stir well.
3. Bring the sauce to a simmer then remove from heat. Let it cool.
4. Pour half of the mixture into a zipper-lock plastic bag then add the chicken thighs to the bag.
5. Seal and shake the plastic bag until the chicken thighs are completely coated with the spices then marinate for 4 hours to 8 hours. Store in the fridge to keep it fresh.
6. After several hours, remove the marinated chicken thighs from the fridge then thaw at room temperature.
7. Next, plug the wood pellet smoker then fill the hopper with the wood pellet. Turn the switch on.
8. Set the wood pellet smoker for indirect heat then adjust the temperature to 275°F (135°C).
9. Arrange the seasoned chicken thighs in the wood pellet smoker then smoke for an hour and 15 minutes.
10. Once the internal temperature of the smoked chicken thighs has reached 170°F (77°C), remove them from the wood pellet smoker.
11. Arrange the smoked chicken thighs on a serving dish then drizzle the remaining sauce on top. Serve and enjoy.

Nutrition: Calories: 297 Carbs: 15g Fat: 8g Protein: 0g

Wood Pellet Smoked Chicken Breasts

Preparation Time: 15 minutes
Cooking Time: 45 minutes
Servings: 4

Ingredients:
- 4 boneless and skinless chicken breasts.
- 1 tablespoon of olive oil.
- 2 tablespoons of brown sugar.
- 2 tablespoons of turbinate sugar.
- 1 teaspoon of celery seeds.
- 2 tablespoons of paprika.
- 2 tablespoons of kosher salt to taste.
- 1 teaspoon of black pepper to taste.
- 1 teaspoon of cayenne pepper.
- 2 tablespoons of garlic powder.
- 2 tablespoons of onion powder.

Directions:
1. Using a large mixing bowl, add in the celery seeds, paprika, cayenne pepper, sugars, garlic powder, onion powder, salt, and pepper to taste then mix properly to combine. Use paper towels to pat the chicken dry then rub all sides with the oil. Add some sprinkles of the mixed rub all over the

chicken breast, wrap the chicken in a plastic bag then set aside in the fridge to rest for about fifteen to thirty minutes.
2. Preheat a Wood Pellet smoker and Grill (the smoker precisely) to smoke for about five minutes then turn the heat to 350 degrees and preheat for about fifteen minutes with the lid closed. Place the spiced/coated chicken on the grill then cook for about twelve to thirteen minutes.
3. Flip the chicken side to side, over and cook for another eight to ten minutes until it attains an internal temperature of 165 degrees F. once cooked, warp the chicken in aluminum foil and let rest for about three to five minutes. Slice and serve.

Nutrition: Calories 327 Fat 9g Carbohydrates 23g Protein 40g

Delicious Chicken Fritters

Preparation Time: 15 minutes
Cooking Time: 45 minutes
Servings: 8

Ingredients:
- 2 teaspoons of baking powder.
- 1 cup of shredded cheddar cheese.
- 1 1/2 lbs. of chicken breast.
- 2 eggs.
- 3/4 cup of almond flour.
- 1 1/2 teaspoon of lemon juice.
- 1 small and sliced.
- 3 tablespoons of mayonnaise.

- Olive oil.
- 2 tablespoons of chopped parsley.
- 2 teaspoons of chicken seasoning.
- 1 tablespoon of chopped scallions.
- 2 tablespoons of sour cream.
- 1 chopped yellow onion.
- 1/3 cup of almond milk.

Directions:

1. Preheat a Wood Pellet smoker and Grill to 425 degrees F, rub the chicken with olive oil then season with half of the chicken seasoning. Place the seasoned chicken on the preheated grill and grill for about twenty-five minutes until it attains an internal temperature of 165 degrees F.
2. Let the cooked chicken rest for a few minutes then pull into smaller pieces with a fork then add into a large mixing bowl. Add in other ingredients like the onion, tomato, eggs, parsley, milk, and cheese then mix everything to combine, set aside.
3. In another mixing bowl, add in the rest of the chicken seasoning, flour, and baking powder then mix properly to combine. Pour the mixture into the bowl containing the pulled chicken mixture then mix everything properly to combine. Cover the mixing bowl with a plastic wrap then refrigerate for about two hours.

4. Using another mixing bowl, add in the mayonnaise, sour cream, scallions, parsley, and lemon juice then mix properly to combine. This makes the serving dip. Feel free to store the dip the refrigerator until ready to be served.
5. Preheat the wood Pellet griddle to medium-low flame then grease the griddle with oil. Make fitters shape out of the chicken mixture, place the fritters on the preheated griddle, and cook for about three to four minutes. Flip the fritters over and cook for another three to four minutes then serve with the dip.

Nutrition: Calories 190 Fat 14.1g Carbohydrates 6.7g Protein 9.1g

Wood Pellet Grilled Chicken Satay

Preparation Time: 15 minutes
Cooking Time: 35 minutes
Servings: 4

Ingredients:
- Marinade
- 1 1/2 pounds of a boneless and skinless chicken breasts or thighs.
- 3/4 cup of coconut milk.
- 2 tablespoons of fish sauce.
- 2 tablespoons of soy sauce.
- 2 tablespoons of lime juice.
- 1/2 teaspoon of kosher salt to taste.
- 1/2 teaspoon of black pepper to taste.
- 1/2 teaspoon of garlic powder.
- 1/4 teaspoon of cayenne pepper.
- Dipping sauce
- 1/2 cup of coconut milk.
- 1/3 cup of peanut butter.
- 2 minced cloves of garlic.
- 1 tablespoon of soy sauce.
- 1 teaspoon of fish sauce.

- 1 tablespoon of lime juice.
- 1/2 tablespoon of swerve sweetener.
- 1 tablespoon of sriracha hot sauce.
- 1 cup of chopped cilantro.

Directions:
1. Properly slice the chicken as desired, preferably lengthwise then add to a Ziploc bag, set aside. Using a large mixing bowl, add in the milk, fish sauce, soy sauce, lime juice, garlic powder, cayenne pepper, salt, and pepper to taste then mix properly to combine. Pour the marinade into the resealable bag then shake properly to coat, refrigerate for about thirty minutes to three hours.
2. To make the dipping sauce, place all its ingredients in a mixing bowl then mix properly to combine, set aside. Preheat a Wood Pellet Smoker and Grill to 350 degrees F, thread the chicken onto skewers then place the skewers on the preheated grill.
3. Cook the chicken satay for about ten to fifteen minutes until it reads 165o F. make sure you flip the chicken occasionally as you cook. Serve with the prepared dipping sauce and enjoy.

Nutrition: Calories 488 Fat 32g Carbohydrates 10g Protein 41g

TURKEY

Turkey Breast

Preparation Time: 12 Hours
Cooking Time: 8 Hours
Servings: 6

Ingredients:

For the Brine:

- 2 pounds turkey breast, deboned
- 2 tablespoons ground black pepper
- ¼ cup salt
- 1 cup brown sugar
- 4 cups cold water

For the BBQ Rub:

- 2 tablespoons dried onions
- 2 tablespoons garlic powder
- ¼ cup paprika
- 2 tablespoons ground black pepper
- 1 tablespoon salt
- 2 tablespoons brown sugar
- 2 tablespoons red chili powder
- 1 tablespoon cayenne pepper
- 2 tablespoons sugar
- 2 tablespoons ground cumin

Directions:

1. Prepare the brine and for this, take a large bowl, add salt, black pepper, and sugar in it, pour in water, and stir until sugar has dissolved.
2. Place turkey breast in it, submerge it completely and let it soak for a minimum of 12 hours in the refrigerator.
3. Meanwhile, prepare the BBQ rub and for this, take a small bowl, place all of its ingredients in it and then stir until combined, set aside until required.
4. Then remove turkey breast from the brine and season well with the prepared BBQ rub.
5. When ready to cook, switch on the Traeger grill, fill the grill hopper with apple-flavored wood pellets, power the grill on by using the control panel, select 'smoke' on the temperature dial,

or set the temperature to 180 degrees F and let it preheat for a minimum of 15 minutes.
6. When the grill has preheated, open the lid, place turkey breast on the grill grate, shut the grill, change the smoking temperature to 225 degrees F, and smoke for 8 hours until the internal temperature reaches 160 degrees F.
7. When done, transfer turkey to a cutting board, let it rest for 10 minutes, then cut it into slices and serve.

Nutrition: Calories: 250 Fat: 5 g Carbs: 31 g Protein: 18 g

Apple wood-Smoked Whole Turkey

Preparation Time: 10 minutes
Cooking Time: 5 hours
Servings: 6

Ingredients:

- 1 (10- to 12-pound) turkey, giblets removed
- Extra-virgin olive oil, for rubbing
- ¼ cup poultry seasoning
- 8 tablespoons (1 stick) unsalted butter, melted
- ½ cup apple juice
- 2 teaspoons dried sage
- 2 teaspoons dried thyme

Directions:

1. Supply your smoker with wood pellets and follow the manufacturer's specific start-up procedure. Preheat, with the lid closed, to 250°F.
2. Rub the turkey with oil and season with the poultry seasoning inside and out, getting under the skin.
3. In a bowl, combine the melted butter, apple juice, sage, and thyme to use for basting.
4. Put the turkey in a roasting pan, place on the grill, close the lid, and grill for 5 to 6 hours, basting every hour, until the skin is

brown and crispy, or until a meat thermometer inserted in the thickest part of the thigh reads 165°F.
5. Let the turkey meat rest for about 15 to 20 minutes before carving.

Nutrition: Calories: 180 Carbs: 3g Fat: 2g Protein: 39g

PORK

Apple Wood Paprika Chili Smoked Pulled Pork

Preparation Time: 20 minutes
Cooking Time: 6 hours 10 minutes
Servings: 8

Ingredients:

- Pork Butt (4-lbs., 1.8-kg.)
- The Rub
- Smoked paprika – 2 ½ tablespoons
- Salt – 1 ½ teaspoons
- White sugar – 2 ½ tablespoons
- Ground cumin – 1 tablespoon
- Chili powder – 1 tablespoon
- Pepper – ¾ tablespoon

- Cayenne pepper – 1 ½ tablespoons
- The Sauce
- Yellow mustard – ¾ cup
- Chili powder – ½ tablespoon
- Brown sugar – 3 tablespoons
- Water – 3 tablespoons
- Soy sauce – ¾ teaspoons
- Unsalted butter – 1 tablespoon
- Liquid smoke – ¾ tablespoon

Directions:

1. Combine the rub ingredients—smoked paprika; salt, white sugar, ground cumin, chili powder, pepper, and cayenne pepper in a bowl then mix well.
2. Apply the rub mixture over the pork butt then set aside.
3. Next, plug the wood pellet smoker then fill the hopper with the wood pellet. Turn the switch on.
4. Set the wood pellet smoker for indirect heat then adjust the temperature to 250°F (121°C).
5. Wait until the wood pellet smoker reaches the desired temperature then place the seasoned pork butt in it.
6. Smoke the pork butt 3 hours or until the internal temperature of the smoked pork butt has reached 165°F (74°C).
7. Take out the smoked pork butt out of the wood pellet smoker then wrap with aluminum foil.
8. After that, return the wrapped smoked pork butt to the wood pellet smoker and continue smoking for another 3 hours.

9. In the meantime, place the entire sauce ingredients—yellow mustard, chili powder, brown sugar, water, soy sauce, unsalted butter, and liquid smoke in a saucepan then bring to a simmer. Remove from heat and set aside.
10. Once the internal temperature of the smoked pork butt has reached 205°F (96°C), take it out of the wood pellet smoker and let it rest for approximately 15 minutes.
11. Unwrap the smoked pork butt then using a fork shred the smoked pork butt.
12. Place the shredded smoked pork butt in a serving dish then drizzle the sauce on top. Mix well.

Nutrition: Calories: 230 Carbs: 1g Fat: 22g Protein: 8g

Bourbon Honey Glazed Smoked Pork Ribs

Preparation Time: 15 minutes
Cooking Time: 5 hours
Servings: 10

Ingredients:

- Pork Ribs (4-lbs., 1.8-kg.)
- The Marinade
- Apple juice – 1 ½ cups
- Yellow mustard – ½ cup
- The Rub
- Brown sugar – ¼ cup
- Smoked paprika – 1 tablespoon
- Onion powder – ¾ tablespoon
- Garlic powder – ¾ tablespoon
- Chili powder – 1 teaspoon
- Cayenne pepper – ¾ teaspoon
- Salt – 1 ½ teaspoons
- The Glaze
- Unsalted butter – 2 tablespoons
- Honey – ¼ cup
- Bourbon – 3 tablespoons

Directions:

1. Place apple juice and yellow mustard in a bowl then stir until combined.
2. Apply the mixture over the pork ribs then marinate for at least an hour.
3. In the meantime, combine brown sugar with smoked paprika, onion powder, garlic powder, chili powder, black pepper, cayenne pepper, and salt then mix well.
4. After an hour of marinade, sprinkle the dry spice mixture over the marinated pork ribs then let it rest for a few minutes.
5. Next, plug the wood pellet smoker then fill the hopper with the wood pellet. Turn the switch on.
6. Set the wood pellet smoker for indirect heat then adjust the temperature to 250°F (121°C).
7. When the wood pellet smoker is ready, place the seasoned pork ribs in the wood pellet smoker and smoke for 3 hours.
8. Meanwhile, place unsalted butter in a saucepan then melt over very low heat.
9. Once it is melted, remove from heat then add honey and bourbon to the saucepan. Stir until incorporated and set aside.
10. After 3 hours of smoking, baste the honey bourbon mixture over the pork ribs and wrap with aluminum foil.
11. Return the wrapped pork ribs to the wood pellet smoker and continue smoking for the next 2 hours.
12. Once the internal temperature of the smoked pork ribs reaches 145°F (63°C), remove the smoked pork ribs from the wood pellet smoker.
13. Unwrap the smoked pork ribs and serve.

Nutrition: Calories: 313 Carbs: 5g Fat: 20g Protein: 26g

Lime Barbecue Smoked Pork Shoulder Chili

Preparation Time: 20 minutes
Cooking Time: 6 hours 10 minutes
Servings: 8

Ingredients:

- Pork Shoulder (3.5-lb., 1.6-kg.)
- The Rub
- Brown sugar – 3 tablespoons
- Garlic powder – 1 tablespoon
- Smoked paprika -1 tablespoon
- Ground cumin – 1 tablespoon
- Salt – 1 teaspoon
- Chili powder – 1 ½ teaspoons
- Black pepper – 1 teaspoon
- The Glaze
- Red chili flakes – 1 tablespoon
- Vegetable oil – 2 tablespoons
- Minced garlic – 1 tablespoon
- Ground coriander – 1 ½ teaspoons
- Tomato ketchup – 1 ½ cups
- White sugar – ¼ cup
- Apple juice – ½ cup
- The Topping

- Fresh limes - 2

Directions:

1. Place brown sugar, garlic powder, smoked paprika, ground cumin, salt, chili powder, and black pepper in a bowl then stir until combined.
2. Rub the spices mixture over and side by side of the pork shoulder then let it rest for approximately an hour.
3. In the meantime, pour vegetable oil into a saucepan then preheat over medium heat.
4. Once the oil is hot, stir in minced garlic and sauté until wilted and aromatic. Remove the saucepan from heat.
5. Stir in red chili flakes, ground coriander, and white sugar into the saucepan then pour apple juice and tomato ketchup over the sauce. Mix well and set aside.
6. Next, plug the wood pellet smoker then fill the hopper with the wood pellet. Turn the switch on.
7. Set the wood pellet smoker for indirect heat then adjust the temperature to 250°F (121°C).
8. Place the seasoned pork shoulder in the wood pellet smoker and smoke for 3 hours. The internal temperature should be 165°F (74°C).
9. Take the pork shoulder out of the wood pellet smoker then place it on a sheet of aluminum foil.
10. Baste the glaze over the pork shoulder then arrange sliced limes over the pork shoulder.

11. Wrap the pork shoulder with aluminum foil then return it to the wood pellet smoker.
12. Smoke the wrapped smoked pork shoulder for another 3 hours or until the internal temperature has reached 205°F (96°C).
13. Once it is done, remove the smoked pork shoulder from the wood pellet smoker and let it rest for approximately 15 minutes.
14. Unwrap the smoked pork shoulder and place it on a serving dish.

Nutrition: Calories: 220 Carbs: 1g Fat: 18g Protein: 16g

Chili Sweet Smoked Pork Tenderloin

Preparation Time: 10 minutes
Cooking Time: 3 hours 30 minutes
Servings: 8

Ingredients:

- Pork Tenderloin (3-lb., 1.4-kg.)
- The Rub
- Apple juice – 1 cup
- Honey – ½ cup
- Brown sugar – ¾ cup
- Dried thyme – 2 tablespoons
- Black pepper – ½ tablespoon
- Chili powder – 1 ½ teaspoons
- Italian seasoning – ½ teaspoon
- Onion powder – 1 teaspoon

Directions:

1. Pour apple juice into a container then stir in honey, brown sugar, dried thyme, black pepper, chili powder, Italian seasoning, and onion powder. Mix well.
2. Rub the pork tenderloin with the spice mixture then let it rest for an hour.

3. Next, plug the wood pellet smoker then fill the hopper with the wood pellet. Turn the switch on.
4. Set the wood pellet smoker for indirect heat then adjust the temperature to 250°F (121°C).
5. When the wood pellet smoker has reached the desired temperature, place the seasoned pork tenderloin in the wood pellet smoker and smoke for 3 hours.
6. After 3 hours of smoking, increase the temperature of the wood pellet smoker to 350°F (177°C) and continue smoking the pork tenderloin for another 30 minutes.
7. Once the internal temperature of the smoked pork tenderloin has reached 165°F (74°C), remove it from the wood pellet smoker and transfer to a serving dish.
8. Cut the smoked pork tenderloin into thick slices then serve.

Nutrition: Calories: 318 Carbs: 7g Fat: 10g Protein: 8g

Gingery Maple Glazed Smoked Pork Ribs

Preparation Time: 15 minutes
Cooking Time: 5 hours 10 minutes
Servings: 8

Ingredients:

- Pork Ribs (4-lbs., 1.8-kg.)
- The Spices
- Apple juice – ¼ cup
- Brown sugar – 3 tablespoons
- Salt – 1 teaspoon
- Black pepper – 1 tablespoon
- Onion powder – ½ tablespoon
- Oregano – 1 tablespoon
- Cayenne pepper – ½ teaspoon
- Chili powder – 1 tablespoon
- The Glaze
- Maple syrup – ¼ cup
- Ginger – 1 teaspoon
- Apple cider vinegar – 1 teaspoon
- Mustard – ½ teaspoon

Directions:

1. Combine brown sugar with salt, black pepper, garlic powder, onion powder, oregano, cayenne pepper then mix well.
2. Baste the pork ribs with the apple juice then sprinkle the dry spice mixture over the pork ribs. Set aside.
3. Next, plug the wood pellet smoker then fill the hopper with the wood pellet. Turn the switch on.
4. Set the wood pellet smoker for indirect heat then adjust the temperature to 250°F (121°C).
5. Place the seasoned pork ribs in the wood pellet smoker and smoke for 5 hours.
6. In the meantime, combine maple syrup with ginger, apple cider vinegar, and mustard. Stir until incorporated and set aside.
7. After 5 hours of smoking, check the smoked pork ribs and once the internal temperature of the smoked pork ribs has reached 145°F (63°C), remove it from the wood pellet smoker.
8. Baste maple syrup mixture over the smoked pork ribs and quickly wrap with aluminum foil.
9. Let the wrapped smoked pork ribs rest for approximately 10 minutes then unwrap and serve it.

Nutrition: Calories: 301 Carbs: 9g Fat: 20g Protein: 23g

Tasty Grilled Pork Chops

Preparation Time: 15 minutes
Cooking Time: 1 hour 30 minutes
Servings: 4

Ingredients:

- 4 pork chops.
- 1/4 cup of olive oil.
- 1 1/2 tablespoons of brown sugar.
- 2 teaspoons of Dijon mustard.
- 1 1/2 tablespoons of soy sauce.
- 1 teaspoon of lemon zest.
- 2 teaspoons of chopped parsley.
- 2 teaspoons of chopped thyme.
- 1/2 teaspoon of salt to taste.
- 1/2 teaspoon of pepper to taste.
- 1 teaspoon of minced garlic.

Directions:

1. Using a small mixing bowl, add in all the ingredients on the list aside from the pork chops then mix properly to combine. This makes the marinade. Place the chops into a Ziploc bag, pour in the prepared marinade then shake properly to coat. Let the pork chops marinate in the refrigerator for about one to eight hours.

2. Next, preheat a Wood Pellet Smoker and Grill to 300 degrees F, place the marinated pork chops on the grill and cook for about six to eight minutes. Flip it side by side of the meat over and cook for an additional six to eight minutes until it attains an internal temperature of 165 degrees F.
3. Once cooked, let the pork chops rest for about five minutes, slice and serve.

Nutrition: Calories 313 Carbohydrate 5g Protein 30g Fat 14g

Delicious Barbeque and Grape Jelly Pork Chops

Preparation Time: 10 minutes
Cooking Time: 30 minutes
Servings: 4

Ingredients:

- 4 boneless pork chops.
- 1/2 cup of barbeque sauce.
- 1/4 cup of grape jelly.
- 2 minced cloves of garlic.
- 1/2 teaspoon of ground black pepper to taste.

Directions:

1. Using a small mixing bowl, add in the barbeque sauce, grape jelly, garlic, and pepper to taste then mix properly to combine. Using a reseal able plastic bag, add in the pork chops alongside with half of the prepared marinade then shake properly to coat. Wait until the pork marinate in the refrigerator for about four to eight hours.
2. Preheat a Wood Pellet Smoker and Grill to 350 degrees F, place the marinated pork chops on the grill, and grill for about six to eight minutes. Flip the pork over, blast with the reserved marinade then grill for an additional six to eight hours until it is

cooked through and attains an internal temperature of 145 degrees F.
3. Once cooked, let the pork rest for about five minutes, slice and serve with your favorite sauce.

Nutrition: Calories 302 Carbohydrates 22g Protein 29g Fat 9g

Bacon Wrapped Jalapeno Poppers

Preparation Time: 10 minutes
Cooking Time: 1 hour 45 minutes
Servings: 8

Ingredients:

- 8 jalapeno peppers.
- 8 ounces of softened cream cheese.
- 1 minced green onion.
- 3/4 teaspoon of garlic powder.
- 1/2 cup of shredded cheddar cheese.
- 16 bacon slices.

Directions:

1. Using a very sharp knife to cut off the steam of each jalapeno then slice lengthwise. Scoop out the seeds, discard then set the jalapenos aside. Using a small mixing bowl, add in the cream cheese, green onion, garlic powder, and cheese then mix properly to combine.
2. Stuff each jalapeno with the cheese mixture then wrap up with a piece of bacon. Make sure to secure the bacon wraps with toothpicks. Place the stuffed jalapenos into the refrigerator and let rest for about one hour. This step will prevent the cheese from melting when grilling.

3. Preheat Wood Pellet Smoker and Grill to 275 degrees F, add in the jalapenos and grill for about forty-five minutes. Just check the doneness of the jalapenos halfway through the cooking process. Serve.

Nutrition: Calories 345 Carbohydrates 3g Protein 11g Fat 32g

Barbeque Baby Back Ribs

Preparation Time: 15 minutes
Cooking Time: 1 hour 30 minutes
Servings: 6

Ingredients:

- 2 racks baby back ribs.
- 3/4 cup of chicken broth.
- 3/4 cup of soy sauce.
- 1 cup of sugar.
- 6 tablespoons of cider vinegar.
- 6 tablespoons of olive oil.
- 3 minced garlic cloves.
- 2 teaspoons of salt to taste.
- 1 tablespoon of paprika.
- 1/2 teaspoon of chili powder.
- 1/2 teaspoon of pepper to taste.
- 1/4 teaspoon of garlic powder.
- A dash of cayenne pepper.
- Barbecue sauce.

Directions:

1. Using a large mixing bowl, add in half of the sugar, soy sauce, vinegar, oil, and garlic then mix properly to combine. This makes the marinade. Place the pork ribs in a Ziploc bag, pour in

about 2/3 of the prepared marinade then sake properly to coat. Allow the ribs marinate in the refrigerator for overnight.
2. Using another mixing bowl, add in the rest of the sugar, salt, and seasonings on the list then mix properly to combine. Rub the ribs with the mixture, coating all sides then set aside. Preheat a Wood Pellet Smoker Grill to 250 degrees F, place the ribs on the preheated grill and grill for about two hours.
3. Blast the ribs with the reserved marinade and cook for an additional one hour. Once cooked, let rest for about five to ten minutes, slice, and serve.

Nutrition: Calories 647 Fat 41g Carbohydrate 30g Protein 37g

Delicious Grilled Pulled Pork

Preparation Time: 15 minutes
Cooking Time: 8 hours 15 minutes
Servings: 6

Ingredients:

- 1 (5 to 6 pounds) boneless pork butt.
- For the Rub:
- 2 tablespoons of paprika.
- 2 teaspoons of salt to taste.
- 2 teaspoons of dried oregano.
- 2 teaspoons of garlic powder.
- 2 teaspoons of dried thyme.
- 1/2 teaspoon of ground red pepper to taste.
- 1/2 teaspoon of ground black pepper to taste.

Directions:

1. Using a small mixing bowl, add in the paprika, oregano, garlic powder, thyme, red pepper, black pepper, and salt to taste then mix properly to combine. Place the pork meat into a large mixing bowl, add in the prepared rub then toss to coat. Cover the mixing bowl with a plastic wrap then let the pork marinate for about one to three hours in the refrigerator.
2. Next, preheat a Wood Pellet Smoker and Grill to 255 degrees F, place pork on the smoker, and cook for about six hours. Wrap

the pork in two pieces of aluminum foil, increase the grill temperature to 250 degrees F and cook the pork for an additional two hours until it is cooked through and tender.
3. Make sure the pork reads an internal temperature of 204 degrees F. Once cooked, let the pork cool for a few minutes, unwarp the foil then shred with a fork. Serve.

Nutrition: Calories 859 Fat 52g Carbohydrate 2g Protein 91g

DESSERT

Cheesy Jalapeño Skillet Dip

Preparation Time: 10 minutes
Cooking Time: 15 minutes
Serving: 8

Ingredients:

- 8 ounces cream cheese
- 16 ounces shredded cheese
- 1/3 cup mayonnaise
- 4 ounces diced green chilies
- 3 fresh jalapeños
- 2 teaspoons Killer Hogs AP Rub
- 2 teaspoons Mexican Style Seasoning

For the topping:

- ¼ cup Mexican Blend Shredded Cheese
- Sliced jalapeños
- Mexican Style Seasoning
- 3 tablespoons Killer Hogs AP Rub
- 2 tablespoons Chili Powder
- 2 tablespoons Paprika
- 2 teaspoons Cumin
- ½ teaspoon Granulated Onion
- ¼ teaspoon Cayenne Pepper
- ¼ teaspoon Chipotle Chili Pepper ground
- ¼ teaspoon Oregano

Directions:

1. Preheat smoker or flame broil for roundabout cooking at 350⁰
2. Join fixings in a big bowl and spot in a cast to press skillet
3. Top with Mexican Blend destroyed cheddar and cuts of jalapeno's
4. Spot iron skillet on flame broil mesh and cook until cheddar hot and bubbly and the top has seared
5. Marginally about 25mins.
6. Serve warm with enormous corn chips (scoops), tortilla chips, or your preferred vegetables for plunging.

Nutrition: Calories: 150 Carbs: 22g Fat: 6g Protein: 3g

Cajun Turkey Club

Preparation Time: 5 Minutes
Cooking Time: 10 Minutes
Servings: 3

Ingredients:

- 1 3lbs Turkey Breast
- 1 stick Butter (melted)
- 8 ounces Chicken Broth
- 1 tablespoon Killer Hogs Hot Sauce
- 1/4 cup Malcolm's King Craw Seasoning
- 8 Pieces to Thick Sliced Bacon
- 1 cup Brown Sugar
- 1 head Green Leaf Lettuce
- 1 Tomato (sliced)
- 6 slices Toasted Bread
- ½ cup Cajun Mayo
- 1 cup Mayo
- 1 tablespoon Dijon Mustard
- 1 tablespoon Killer Hogs Sweet Fire Pickles (chopped)
- 1 tablespoon Horseradish
- ½ teaspoon Malcolm's King Craw Seasoning
- 1 teaspoon Killer Hogs Hot Sauce
- Pinch of Salt & Black Pepper to taste

Directions:

1. Get ready pellet smoker for backhanded cooking at 325⁰ utilizing your preferred wood pellets for enhancing.
2. Join dissolved margarine, chicken stock, hot sauce, and 1 Tbl-Spn of Cajun Seasoning in a blending bowl. Infuse the blend into the turkey bosom scattering the infusion destinations for even inclusion.
3. Shower the outside of the turkey bosom with a Vegetable cooking splash and season with Malcolm's King Craw Seasoning.
4. Spot the turkey bosom on the smoker and cook until the inside temperature arrives at 165⁰. Utilize a moment read thermometer to screen temp during the cooking procedure.
5. Consolidate darker sugar and 1 teaspoon of King Craw in a little bowl. Spread the bacon with the sugar blend and spot on a cooling rack.
6. Cook the bacon for 12 to 15mins or until darker. Make certain to turn the bacon part of the way through for cooking.
7. Toast the bread, cut the tomatoes dainty, and wash/dry the lettuce leaves.
8. At the point when the turkey bosom arrives at 165 take it from the flame broil and rest for 15mins. Take the netting out from around the bosom and cut into slender cuts.
9. To cause the sandwich: To slather Cajun Mayo* on the toast, stack on a few cuts of turkey bosom, lettuce, tomato, and bacon. Include another bit of toast and rehash a similar procedure.

Include the top bit of toast slathered with more Cajun mayo, cut the sandwich into equal parts and appreciate.

Nutrition: Calories: 130 Carbs: 1g Fat: 4g Protein: 21g

RUBS, SAUCES, MARINADES, AND GLAZES

Three Pepper Rub

Preparation Time: 10 minutes
Cooking Time: 3 Hours
Servings: 3

Ingredients:

- 2 tablespoons of black pepper
- 2 tablespoons of white pepper
- 2 tablespoons of red pepper
- 1 tablespoon of onion powder
- 2 teaspoons of garlic powder
- 2 tablespoons of dried thyme
- 4 tablespoons of paprika
- 2 tablespoons of dried oregano

Directions:

1. Mix all the spices in the bowl and transfer to aluminum foil tin.
2. Preheat the smoker grill at 220 degrees F for 20 minutes.
3. Put the aluminum foil tin onto the grill grate and smoke for 3 hours by closing the lid.
4. Once done, store it in the tight jar for further use.

Nutrition: Calories: 67 Carbs: 16g Fat: 2g Protein: 2g

Jerky Seasoning

Preparation Time: 10 minutes
Cooking Time: 2 Hours
Servings: 4

Ingredients:
- 8 tablespoons dried minced onion
- 6 teaspoons dried thyme
- 4 teaspoons ground allspice
- 2 teaspoons ground black pepper
- 4 teaspoons ground cinnamon
- 4 teaspoons cayenne pepper
- 2 teaspoons sea salt

Directions:
1. Mix all the spices in the bowl, and transfer to aluminum foil tin.
2. Preheat the smoker grill to 220 degrees F, by closing the lid for 22 minutes.
3. Place the aluminum foil pan onto the smoker grill grate, and let it smoke for 2 hours.
4. The spices will be smoked to perfection until now.
5. Let the spices get cool down before storing in the airtight jars.

Nutrition: Calories: 63 Carbs: 0g Fat: 1g Protein: 13g

Not-Just-For-Pork Rub

Preparation Time: 5 minutes
Cooking Time: 0 minute
Servings: 4

Ingredients:
- ½ teaspoon ground thyme
- ½ teaspoon paprika
- ½ teaspoon coarse kosher salt
- ½ teaspoon garlic powder
- ½ teaspoon onion powder
- ½ teaspoon chili powder
- ¼ teaspoon dried oregano leaves
- ¼ teaspoon freshly ground black pepper
- ¼ teaspoon ground chipotle chili pepper
- ¼ teaspoon celery seed

Directions:
1. Using an airtight bag, combine the thyme, paprika, salt, garlic powder, onion powder, chili powder, oregano, black pepper, chipotle pepper, and celery seed. Close the container and shake to mix. Unused rub will keep in an airtight container for months.

Nutrition: Calories: 64 Carbs: 10g Fat: 1g Protein: 1g

Chicken Rub

Preparation Time: 5 minutes
Cooking Time: 0 minute
Servings: 4

Ingredients:
- 2 tablespoons packed light brown sugar
- 1½ teaspoons coarse kosher salt
- 1¼ teaspoons garlic powder
- ½ teaspoon onion powder
- ½ teaspoon freshly ground black pepper
- ½ teaspoon ground chipotle chili pepper
- ½ teaspoon smoked paprika
- ¼ teaspoon dried oregano leaves
- ¼ teaspoon mustard powder
- ¼ teaspoon cayenne pepper

Directions:
1. Using an airtight bag, combine the brown sugar, salt, garlic powder, onion powder, black pepper, chipotle pepper, paprika, oregano, mustard, and cayenne. Close the container and shake to mix. Unused rub will keep in an airtight container for months.

Nutrition: Calories: 15 Carbs: 3g Fat: 0g Protein: 0g

- PART 2 -

ELECTRIC SMOKER COOKBOOK

The smoke outlet is a hole in the top of the smoker. Also, there will be a tray that collects the drops of fat and grease. This tray will need to be emptied after the cooking process is complete.

They are also easy to use, which is probably the biggest reason they are becoming more popular. Unlike other smokers, electric smokers don't have to be monitored at all times. They don't need to be held up to burn a fire on the bottom. Everything is done for them once they are plugged in. The smoking process and the results people get are very enjoyable. Many different types of meats and vegetables can be cooked with this type of smoker. They are very popular with most people because they are relatively inexpensive and easy to use.

APPETIZERS, VEGETABLES, AND SIDES

Twice-Baked Spaghetti Squash

Preparation time: 15 minutes.

Cooking time: 45 minutes.

Servings: 2

Ingredients:

- 1 spaghetti squash, medium
- 1 tablespoon olive oil, extra-virgin
- 1 teaspoon salt
- ½ teaspoon pepper
- ½ cup Parmesan cheese, grated, divided
- ½ cup mozzarella cheese, shredded, divided

Directions:

1. Cut the squash lengthwise in half. Make sure you're using a knife that's large enough and sharp enough. Once you're done, take out the pulp and the seeds from each half with a spoon.

2. Season the insides of each half of the squash with some olive oil. When you're done with that, sprinkle the salt and pepper.

3. Heat your grill to 375°F with your preferred wood pellets.

4. Put each half of the squash on the grill. Make sure they're both facing upwards on the grill grates, which should be nice and hot.

5. Bake for 45minutes, keeping it on the grill until the internal temperature of the squash hits 170°F. You'll know you're done when you find it easy to pierce the squash with a fork.

6. Move the squash to your cutting board. Rest for 10minutes, so it can cool a bit.

7. Turn up the temp on your wood pellet smoker grill to 425°F.

8. Using a fork to remove the flesh from the squash in strands by raking it back and forth. Be careful because you want the shells to remain intact. The strands you rake off should look like spaghetti, if you're doing it right.

9. Put the spaghetti squash strands in a large bowl, and then add in half of your mozzarella and half of your Parmesan cheeses. Combine them by stirring.

10. Take the mix, and stuff it into the squash shells. When you're done, sprinkle them with the rest of the Parmesan and mozzarella cheeses.

11. **Optional:** You can top these with some bacon bits, if you like.

12. Allow the stuffed spaghetti squash shells you've now stuffed to bake at 435°F for 15 minutes.

13. Serve and enjoy.

Nutrition: Calories: 214 **Fat:** 3g **Cholesterol:** 17mg **Carbs:** 27g **Protein:** 16g

Bacon-Wrapped Asparagus

Preparation time: 15 minutes.

Cooking time: 30 minutes.

Servings: 6

Ingredients:

- 15–20 spears of fresh asparagus (1-pound)
- Olive oil, extra-virgin
- 5 slices bacon, thinly sliced
- 1 teaspoon salt and pepper or your preferred rub

Directions:

1. Break off the ends of the asparagus, then trim it all, so they're down to the same length.
2. Separate the asparagus into bundles—3 spears per bundle. Then spritz them with some olive oil.
3. Use a piece of bacon to wrap up each bundle. When you're done, lightly dust the wrapped bundle with some salt and pepper to taste or your preferred rub.

4. Set up your wood pellet smoker grill so that it's ready for indirect cooking.

5. Put some fiberglass mats on your grates. Make sure they're the fiberglass kind. This will keep your asparagus from getting stuck on your grill gates.

6. Heat your grill to 400°F, with whatever pellets you prefer. You can do this as you prep your asparagus.

7. Grill the wraps for 25 minutes to 30minutes, tops. The goal is to get your asparagus looking nice and tender and the bacon deliciously crispy.

Nutrition: Calories: 71 **Fat:** 3g **Carbs**: 1g **Protein:** 6g

Garlic Parmesan Wedges

Preparation time: 15 minutes.

Cooking time: 35 minutes.

Servings: 3

Ingredients:

- 3 russet potatoes, large
- 2 teaspoons garlic powder
- ¾ teaspoon black pepper
- 1(½) teaspoons salt
- ¾ cup Parmesan cheese, grated
- 3 tablespoons fresh cilantro, chopped, optional. You can replace this with flat-leaf parsley
- ½ cup blue cheese per serving, as an optional dip. Can be replaced with ranch dressing
- Olive oil
- Garlic

Directions:

1. Use some cold water to scrub your potatoes as gently as you can with a veggie brush. When done, let them dry.

2. Slice your potatoes along the length in half. Cut each half into a third.

3. Get all the extra moisture off your potato by wiping it all away with a paper towel. If you don't do this, then you're not going to have crispy wedges!

4. In a large bowl, throw in your potato wedges, some olive oil, garlic powder, salt, garlic, and pepper, and then toss them with your hands lightly. You want to make sure the spices and oil get on every wedge.

5. Place your wedges on a nonstick grilling tray, pan, or basked. The single-layer kind. Make sure it's at least 15 x 12 inches.

6. Set up your wood pellet smoker grill, so it's ready for indirect cooking.

7. Heat your grill to 425°F, with whatever wood pellets you like.

8. Set the grilling tray upon your heated grill. Roast the wedges for 15minutes before you flip them. Once you turn

them, roast them for another 15minutes, or 20 tops. The outside should be a nice, crispy, golden brown.

9. Sprinkle your wedges generously with the Parmesan cheese. When you're done, garnish it with some parsley or cilantro, if you like. Serve these bad boys up with some ranch dressing, some blue cheese, or just eat them that way!

Nutrition: Calories: 194 **Fat:** 5g **Cholesterol:** 5mg **Carbs**: 32g **Protein:** 5g

BEEF

Savory Smoked Beef Chuck Roast with Red Wine Sauce

Preparation time: 10 minutes.

Cooking time: 6 hours.

Servings: 10

Ingredients:

- 4-pound (1.8-kilograms) beef chuck roast

The rub:

- 1(¼) tablespoons Kosher salt
- 1 teaspoon pepper

The sauce:

- 2 tablespoons olive oil
- 1 teaspoon onion powder
- 1(½) teaspoons garlic powder
- 2 bay leaves
- ½ cup dried red wine

- 1(½) teaspoons balsamic vinegar
- 2 teaspoons Worcestershire sauce
- 2 teaspoons soy sauce
- ½ cup beef broth
- Brown sugar, a pinch

Directions:

1. Rub the beef chuck roast with salt and pepper, then set aside.
2. Pour beef broth and olive oil into a heavy-duty aluminum pan, then add onion powder, garlic powder, dried red wine, balsamic vinegar, Worcestershire sauce, soy sauce, and brown sugar. Stir the sauce until incorporated.
3. Next, plug in the Electric Smoker and press the power button to turn it on.
4. Press the "Temperature" button and set it to 225°F (107°C).
5. After that, add wood chips to the smoker and pour beer into the water pan.

6. Place the seasoned beef chuck roast in the aluminum pan with sauce and flip until all sides of the beef chuck roast are completely coated with the sauce mixture.

7. Once the Electric Smoker is ready, place the aluminum pan with beef chuck roast in it and set the time to 6 hours. Smoke the beef chuck roast.

8. Regularly check the temperature of the Electric Smoker and add more wood chips if it is necessary.

9. Check the internal temperature of the smoked beef chuck roast and once it reaches 125°F (52°C), remove it from the Electric Smoker.

10. Place the smoked beef chuck roast on a serving dish, then drizzle the sauce on top.

11. Serve and enjoy warm.

Butter Garlic Smoked Beef Rib Eye Rosemary

Preparation time: 10 minutes

Cooking time: 3 hours

Servings: 10

Ingredients:

- 5-pound (2.3-kilograms) beef rib eye

The rub:

- 3 tablespoons minced garlic
- ½ teaspoon grated lemon zest
- 1 teaspoon dried thyme
- 1 teaspoon dried rosemary
- 1 teaspoon dried basil
- ¾ teaspoon Kosher salt
- ½ teaspoon black pepper

The topping:

- 1 cup cold butter cubes

Directions:

1. Rub the beef rib eye with minced garlic, grated lemon zest, dried thyme, dried rosemary, dried basil, kosher salt, and black pepper, then place in a heavy-duty aluminum pan.

2. Sprinkle cold butter cubes over the seasoned beef rib eye and put fresh rosemary on top.

3. Plug in the Electric Smoker and press the power button to turn it on.

4. Press the "Temperature" button and set it to 225°F (107°C).

5. After that, add wood chips to the smoker and pour water into the water pan. Add fresh rosemary to the water pan.

6. When the Electric Smoker is ready, place the aluminum pan in it, then smoke the seasoned beef rib eye.

7. Set the time to 3hours and once the internal temperature of the smoked beef rib eye has reached 125°F (52°C), remove it from the Electric Smoker.

8. Place the smoked beef rib eye on a serving dish, then serve.

9. Enjoy warm.

Nutrition:

Calcium: 47mg **Magnesium:** 43mg **Phosphorus:** 452mg **Iron:** 5.38mg **Potassium:** 769mg **Sodium:** 505mg **Zinc:** 17.89mg

Oak-Smoked Top Round

Preparation time: 10 minutes.

Cooking time: 5 hours.

Servings: 12

Ingredients:

- 12 hamburger buns
- 1 beef top round
- 3 tablespoon melted butter
- Kosher salt, black pepper

Directions:

1. Add oak wood chips to the Wood Chips box, then plug the smoker and heat it to 275°F.

2. Coat the meat with salt and pepper on the meat. Transfer the meat to the cooking grates and allow to smoke for about 5 hours. Or when the internal temperature of the beef records 145°F.

3. Transfer the meat to an aluminum foil. Let it rest for about 15–20minutes. Brush the sides with melted butter.

4. Slice the meat thinly on the buns. Serve immediately.

Nutrition:

Calories: 310kcal **Carbs:** 32g **Fat:** 50g **Protein:** 46.5g

LAMB

Garlic Mint Smoked Lamb Chops Balsamic

Preparation time: 10 minutes.

Cooking time: 4 hours.

Servings: 10

Ingredients:

- 6-pound (2.7-kilograms) lamb chops

The rub:

- 1 teaspoon dried mint leaves
- ¼ cup olive oil
- ¼ cup minced garlic
- 1 teaspoon black pepper
- 1 teaspoon dried rosemary
- ½ teaspoon oregano
- ½ teaspoon dried thyme
- 1(½) teaspoon Kosher salt

The glaze:

- 1 cup balsamic vinegar
- 6 tablespoons brown sugar
- ½ teaspoon black pepper

Directions:

1. Combine the rub ingredients—dried mint leaves, olive oil, minced garlic, black pepper, dried rosemary, oregano, dried thyme, and kosher salt, then stir well.

2. Rub the lamb with the spice mixture, then set aside.

3. Turn the Electric Smoker on, then set the temperature to 225°F (107°C).

4. Wait until the Electric Smoker has reached the desired temperature, then add wood chips to the chip tray. Pour water into the water pan.

5. Put the seasoned lamb chops on the grill tray provided by the Electric Smoker and smoke for 2hours.

6. Combine balsamic vinegar with brown sugar and black pepper, then stir until incorporated.

7. After 2hours, transfer the lamb chops to a disposable aluminum pan, then drizzle the balsamic vinegar mixture over the lamb chops.

8. Continue smoking the lamb chops for another 2 hours or until the internal temperature of the smoked lamb chops has reached 135°F (57°C).

9. Remove the smoked lamb chops from the Electric Smoker, then transfer to a serving dish.

10. Serve and enjoy.

Nutrition:

Calcium: 58mg **Magnesium:** 66mg **Phosphorus:** 520mg **Iron:** 4.35mg **Potassium:** 923mg **Sodium:** 216mg **Zinc:** 7.34mg

CHICKEN

American Style Chicken Thighs

Preparation time: 15 minutes.

Cooking time: 2 hours.

Servings: 6

Ingredients:

- 6 (6-ounce) skinless, boneless chicken thighs
- 6 cups water
- 1 (12-ounce) can beer
- ¼ cup brown sugar
- ¼ cup kosher salt

For rub:

- 2 tablespoon brown sugar
- 2 tablespoon cornstarch
- ½ teaspoon cayenne pepper
- Salt and freshly ground black pepper

Directions:

1. In a large bowl, add water, beer, brown sugar and salt and mix until sugar is dissolved.

2. Add the chicken thighs and mix well.

3. Cover and refrigerate overnight.

4. Remove the chicken thighs from the brine and with paper towels, pat them dry.

5. Heat the smoker to 180°F, using charcoal.

6. **For the rub:** in a bowl, mix together all the ingredients.

7. Rub the chicken with the mixture generously.

8. Place the chicken thighs into the smoker and cook for about 1 hour.

9. Now, set the temperature of the smoker to 350°F and cook for about ¾–1 hour

Nutrition:

Energy: 178kcal **Carbohydrate:** 12.54g **Calcium:** 129mg **Magnesium:** 19mg **Phosphorus:** 133mg **Iron:** 0.48mg **Potassium:** 148mg

Smoked Chicken Cutlets In Strawberries-Balsamic Marinade

Preparation time: 2 hours.

Cooking time: 2 hours, 15 minutes.

Servings: 6

Ingredients:

- 3 tablespoon balsamic vinegar
- 20 medium strawberries
- 1/4 cup extra-virgin olive oil
- 2 tablespoon chopped fresh basil
- Kosher salt and freshly ground black pepper
- 2 pounds boneless, skinless chicken breast cutlets

Directions:

1. Whisk balsamic vinegar, strawberries, olive oil, and fresh basil in your blender.

2. Sprinkle marinade on and rub into the tops, bottoms, and sides of the chicken cutlets.

3. Refrigerate for 2 hours.

4. Heat Electric Smoker. Allow the smoker temperature to reach 225°F.

5. When it is ready, add some water to the removable pan that is usually on the bottom shelf.

6. Fill the side "drawer" with dry wood chips.

7. Smoke chicken for about two hours or until the internal temperature reaches 165°F.

8. Serve hot.

Nutrition:

Calories: 127 **Total fat:** 9g **Saturated fat:** 1.2g **Cholesterol:** 22mg **Sodium:** 26mg **Total carbohydrate:** 3.2g **Dietary fiber:** 0.8g **Total sugars:** 2g **Protein:** 9g **Vitamin D:** 0mcg **Calcium:** 15mg **Iron:** 0mg **Potassium:** 69mg

Beer Can Chicken

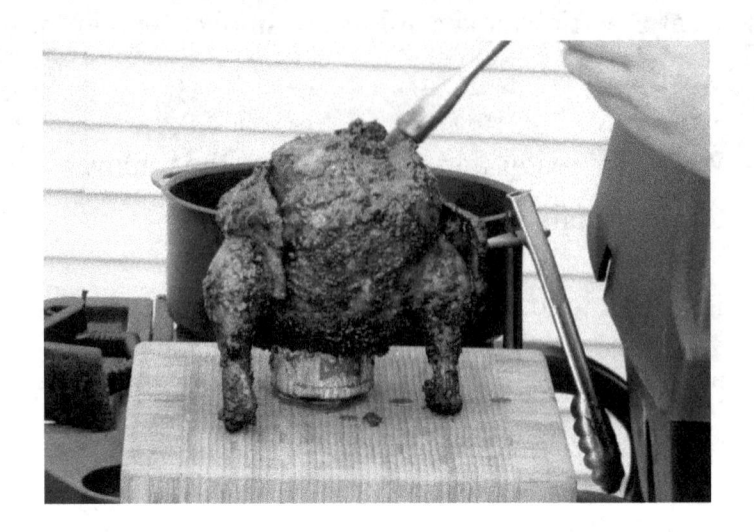

Preparation time: 5 minutes.

Cooking time: 3–4 hours.

Servings: 4

Ingredients:

- 1 can (12 ounces) beer
- 2 tablespoons apple cider vinegar
- 2 garlic cloves (minced)
- 1 whole chicken (4 to 5 pounds)

- 1 to 2 teaspoons chili powder
- 1 teaspoon salt
- 1 teaspoon onion powder
- 1/2 teaspoon freshly ground black pepper

Directions:

1. Pour 2 cups of water into the smoker's water pan. Place oak or pecan wood chips in the smoker's wood tray and heat the smoker to 225°F.

2. Drink half of the can of beer. Pop two more holes in the top of the can with a can opener. Add apple cider vinegar and garlic to beer and set aside until beer comes to room temperature.

3. Remove gizzards and neck from chicken cavity if necessary. Rinse chicken inside and out with cold water and pat dry with paper towels. Mix chili powder, salt, onion powder, and pepper and rub over inside and outside of the chicken.

4. Set the beer can on a sturdy surface and slide the chicken cavity over the can so the chicken is standing up. Transfer the chicken with the can onto the smoker grate and smoke until the internal temperature of the meat reaches

165°F, 3 to 4 hours. Add wood chips to the wood tray as necessary.

5. Remove the chicken from the smoker and remove the can. Cover chicken loosely with aluminum foil and let rest for about 10 minutes. Carve chicken as desired, serve and enjoy!

Nutrition:

Calories 116 **Total Fat** 2.8g **Saturated Fat** 0.8g **Cholesterol** 32mg **Sodium** 624mg **Total Carbohydrate** 4.7g **Dietary Fiber** 0.4g **Total Sugars** 0.3g **Protein** 11.2g **Vitamin D** 0mcg **Calcium** 18mg **Iron** 1mg **Potassium** 146mg

TURKEY

Turkey with Chimichurri

Preparation time: 1 hour, 10 minutes.

Cooking time: 4 hours.

Servings: 5

Ingredients:

- 5 pounds bone-in, skin-on turkey pieces
- Salt and pepper
- 1teaspoon paprika
- ½ teaspoon cayenne
- 2 tablespoons olive oil
- 1 pepper
- 1 onion
- 2 carrots, chopped
- 2 scallions
- 2 tomatoes, chopped

Homemade chimichurri sauce:

- ½ cup olive oil
- 1 teaspoon parsley
- 1 teaspoon red pepper flakes
- 2 garlic cloves
- 2 red onions

Directions:

1. Season the washed and clean turkey with salt, pepper, paprika, and cayenne pepper.
2. Rub it gently all over.
3. Arrange the wood chip inside the smoker and heat the smoker to 230°F.
4. Transfer the turkey to the sheet pan and arrange peppers, onions, carrots, scallion, and tomatoes beside it.
5. Drizzle the olive oil on top.
6. Place the pan sheet inside the smoker.
7. Close the electric smoker door and then cook for 4 hours at 250°F.

8. Check the turkey to an internal temperature of 165°F.

9. Now, it is time to make the chimichurri.

10. Blend all the homemade chimichurri ingredients in a blender and puree until combined.

11. Serve the cooked turkey and veggie with the sauce.

Nutrition:

Calories: 807 **Total fat:** 35.9g **Saturated fat:** 4.5g **Cholesterol:** 283mg **Sodium:** 920mg **Total carbohydrate:** 11.7g **Dietary fiber:** 2.9g **Total sugars:** 5.8g **Protein:** 94.8g **Calcium:** 32mg **Iron:** 6mg 35 **Potassium:** 311mg

PORK

Smoked Boston Butt Roast

Preparation time: 20 minutes.

Cooking time: 4 hours.

Servings: 6

Ingredients:

- 1(5-pounds) pork butt roast
- 4 teaspoon house seasoning, recipe follows
- 2 teaspoon seasoned salt
- 1 medium onion, sliced
- 1 cup water
- 3 bay leaves
- Sweet or Smoky BBQ sauce

House Seasoning:

- 1 cup salt
- 1/4 cup black pepper
- 1/4 cup garlic powder

Directions:

1. On one side of your roast, sprinkle two teaspoon of the House Seasoning. Be sure to rub it in well with your fingers. Flip your roast over and rub in the remaining two teaspoon of the House Seasoning. Repeat this process with your seasoned salt.

2. Place your roast on a large pan for roasting. Add in the bay leaves, onion, and water. Place the roast in your smoker for 4 hours.

3. The internal temperature for the meat should be 170°F. Once it is, allow it to cool for a few minutes.

1. Serve this roast with sweet or smoky BBQ sauce.

Nutrition:

Calcium: 31mg **Magnesium:** 42mg **Phosphorus:** 342mg **Iron:** 1.58mg **Potassium:** 596mg

Smoked Pork Shoulder

Preparation time: 30 minutes.

Cooking time: 5 hours, 30 minutes.

Servings: 6

Ingredients:

- 1(5–6pound) pork shoulder/Boston butt pork roast
- 2 teaspoon salt
- Sweet BBQ Sauce

Directions:

1. Season with salt your pork shoulder. Close it up and chill it in the fridge for half an hour.
2. Place the pork inside the smoker. Close the lid.
3. Cook the meat for Five and a half hours. The temperature of your pork inside should be 165°F. Rotate the pork over for the last two hours of its smoking.
4. Remove the pork, give it a few minutes to cool. Serve with sweet BBQ sauce.

Nutrition:

Calcium: 101mg **Magnesium:** 89mg **Phosphorus:** 809mg **Iron:** 6.81mg **Potassium:** 1186mg **Sodium:** 890mg

Smoked Pork Sausage

Preparation time: 60 minutes.

Cooking time: 3 hours.

Servings: 30 sausage.

Ingredients:

- 20 pounds of home-dressed lean pork meat
- 10 pounds of clear fat pork
- 1/2 pound fine salt (best quality)
- 2 teaspoon sugar
- 1 tablespoon ginger
- 2 teaspoon pepper
- 1 tablespoon sage
- 2 teaspoon cure (either Instacure #1 or Prague Powder #1)

Directions:

1. Cut the meat into cubes. Grind them all together in an extra-large bowl with the spices.

2. Using a sausage grinder, pass the mixed meat and spices through a medium plate on the grinder.

3. Stuff the sausages in natural pork casings so you'll be able to smoke them.

4. Place them in the smoker.

Nutrition:

Calcium, Ca55 mg **Magnesium**, Mg103 mg **Phosphorus**, P1260 mg **Iron**, Fe5.27 mg **Potassium**, K1529 mg

SEAFOOD

Smoked Red Fish Fillets

Preparation time: 16 hours.

Cooking time: 1 hour.

Servings: 2

Ingredients:

- 2 fillets of redfish with skin, each about 12 ounces
- 1 teaspoon garlic powder
- 1/2 cup salt
- 1 teaspoon ground black pepper
- 1/2 cup brown sugar
- 1 teaspoon dried lemon zest
- 1 lemon, sliced

Directions:

1. Stir together garlic powder, salt, black pepper, sugar, and lemon zest until combined.

2. Take a glass baking dish, spread 1/3 of prepared spice mixture in the bottom, then later with one fillet, skin-side down and press lightly.

3. Sprinkle half of the remaining spice mixture over the fillet in the pan, then top with another filet, flesh-side down and then sprinkle the remaining spice mixture on top of it and around the side of the fish.

4. Close the dish with plastic wrap and then let marinate in the refrigerator for 8 to 12 hours.

5. Remove marinated fish from the dish, rinse well, and pat dry using paper towels.

6. Return fish into the refrigerator for 2 to 3 hours or until dried and then bring fish to room temperature for 45 minutes.

7. When ready to cook, plug in the smoker, fill its tray with hickory wood chips and water pan halfway through, and place the dripping pan above the water pan.

8. Then open the top vent, shut with lid and use temperature settings to heat the smoker at 120°F.

9. Place fish on smoker rack, insert a meat thermometer, then shut with lid and set the timer to smoke for 1 hour or

more until meat thermometer registers an internal temperature of 140°F.

10. Check vent of smoker every hour and add more wood chips and water to maintain temperature and smoke.

11. Serve straight away.

Nutrition:

Calories: 27 **Carbs:** 0g **Fat:** 0.5g **Protein:** 5.3g **Fiber:** 0g

Lemon Pepper Tuna

Preparation time: 1 hour.

Cooking time: 4 hours, 10 minutes.

Servings: 6

Ingredients:

- 6 tuna steaks, each about 6 ounces
- 3 tablespoons salt
- 3 tablespoons brown sugar
- 1/4 cup olive oil
- ¼ cup lemon pepper seasoning
- 1 teaspoon minced garlic
- 12 slices of lemon

Directions:

1. Season tuna with salt and sugar until evenly coated on all sides, then place in a dish and cover with plastic wrap.

2. Place dish into the refrigerator for 4 hours or overnight, then rinse well and pat dry and coat well with garlic powder, lemon pepper seasoning, and oil.

3. Plug in the smoker, fill its tray with peach wood chips and water pan halfway through, and place the dripping pan above the water pan.

4. Then open the top vent, shut with lid and use temperature settings to heat the smoker at 120°F.

5. In the meantime, place seasoned tuna on smoker rack, insert a meat thermometer, then shut with lid and set the timer to smoke for 1 hour or more until meat thermometer registers an internal temperature of 140°F.

6. Check vent of smoker every hour and add more wood chips and water to maintain temperature and smoke.

7. When done, transfer tuna to a cutting board, let rest for 10 minutes and then serve with lemon slices.

Nutrition:

Calories: 275 Cal **Carbs:** 0.6g **Fat:** 23 g **Protein:** 17 g **Fiber:** 0 g.

Seasoned Shrimp Skewers

Preparation time: 10 minutes.

Cooking time: 35 minutes.

Servings: 4

Ingredients:

- 1(½) pound fresh large shrimp, peeled, deveined and rinsed
- 2 tablespoons minced basil
- 2 teaspoons minced garlic
- 1/2 teaspoon sea salt
- 1/2 teaspoon ground black pepper
- 1/3 cup olive oil
- 2 tablespoons lemon juice

Directions:

1. Place basil, garlic, salt, black pepper and oil in a large bowl, whisk until well combined, then add shrimps and toss until well coated.

2. Fill the smoker tray with hickory wood chips and water pan with water and white wine halfway through, and place the dripping pan above the water pan.

3. Then open the top vent, shut with lid and use temperature settings to heat the smoker at 225°F.

4. Thread shrimps on wooden skewers, six shrimps on each skewer.

5. Place shrimp skewers on smoker rack, then shut with lid and set the timer to smoke for 35 minutes or shrimps are opaque.

6. When done, drizzle lemon juice over shrimps and serve.

Nutrition:

Calories: 168 **Carbs:** 2g **Fat:** 11g **Protein:** 14g **Fiber:** 0g

RUBS, SAUCES, MARINADES, AND GLAZES

Mustard Sauce for Pork

Preparation time: 5 minutes.

Cooking time: 27 minutes.

Servings: 4 cups

Ingredients:

- 1 cup yellow mustard
- ½ cup balsamic vinegar
- 1/3 cup brown sugar
- 2 tablespoons butter
- 1 tablespoon fresh lemon juice
- 2 teaspoons Worcestershire sauce
- ½ teaspoon chili powder

Directions:

1. Put all the ingredients in a saucepan.

2. Heat until simmering, stirring.

3. Reduce the heat to low after 1–2 minutes of a light boil, then simmer for 25 minutes.

4. Cool to room temperature before storing for 3–4 days in the fridge, or use right away!

Nutrition:

Total calories: 148 **Protein:** 2.8g **Carbs:** 16g **Fat:** 8.3g **Fiber:** 2.1g

Spicy-Citrus Cocktail Sauce

Preparation time: 5 minutes.

Cooking time: 6 minutes.

Servings: 1 ¼ cups.

Ingredients:

- 1 cup ketchup
- ¼ cup orange juice
- 1 minced chipotle chile, jarred in adobo
- 2 tablespoons diced onion
- 1 tablespoon Worcestershire sauce
- 2 teaspoons adobo sauce
- 2 teaspoons dry cilantro
- 1 teaspoon orange zest
- Pinch of red pepper flakes, or more

Directions:

1. Prepare the ingredients in a saucepan, then heat on medium.

2. When simmering, reduce heat, so the sauce is barely bubbling.

3. Cook for 5–6 minutes to blend flavors.

4. Let it rest at room temperature before storing in the fridge.

5. You can serve cocktail sauce cold or warm.

Nutrition: Total calories: 58 **Protein:** 0.9g **Carbs:** 14.6g **Fat:** 0.2g **Fiber:** 0.2g